D0418264

Scotland and the *Slave Trade*

2007 Bicentenary of the
Abolition of the Slave Trade Act

A L I S
1875047

Scottish Executive, Edinburgh 2007

Acknowledgements

The Scottish Executive is grateful to Eric Graham and Iain Whyte for the research which informs this document and to Paula Kitching for conducting further research and authoring the final text. The depth to which issues could be discussed was limited as this publication is intended to provide a short overview of Scotland and the slave trade and a starting point for further exploration.

The views expressed in this document are those of the author and do not necessarily represent those of Scottish Ministers.

306.
362

© Crown copyright 2007

ISBN 978-0-7559-5325-7

Scottish Executive
St Andrew's House
Edinburgh
EH1 3DG

Produced for the Scottish Executive by RR Donnelley B49767 03/07

Published by the Scottish Executive, March, 2007

Further copies are available from
Blackwell's Bookshop
53 South Bridge
Edinburgh
EH1 1YS

The text pages of this document are printed on recycled paper and are 100% recyclable

Contents

Introduction

The detailed history of the transatlantic slave trade is unfamiliar to the majority of the Scottish public. It was a period that lasted for nearly 250 years, affecting generations of people, but a period that is often dismissed.

Credit: The Kneeling Slave - 'Am I not a Man & a Brother' (oil on canvas) by English School (18th century) © Wilberforce House, Hull City Museums and Art Galleries, UK / The Bridgeman Art Library
Nationality / copyright status: English / out of copyright

Chapter 1: Introduction

The detailed history of the transatlantic slave trade is unfamiliar to the majority of the Scottish public. It was a period that lasted for nearly 250 years, affecting generations of people, but a period that is often dismissed. Although most people are appalled by the thought of slavery, there is also the attitude that it happened so long ago, that it was an 'American thing' and that very few British people had anything to do with it. The truth is it is only 200 years since the trade ended and even less since slavery was abolished in the British Empire. **British ships carried just over 3.4 million Africans to slavery in the Caribbean and America.**

(David Richardson, *The British Empire and the Atlantic Slave Trade, 1660 – 1807* in *The Oxford History of the British Empire*, vol.2, *The 18th Century*, edited by P.J. Marshall (Oxford, 1998), 440-464; 441).

Slavery in mainland America and in the Caribbean was introduced and practised by Europeans who had established plantations and wanted cheap labour. London, Liverpool and Bristol were the main ports for the beginning and end of slaving voyages. However, other smaller ports also had their involvement such as Greenock and Glasgow. Most significantly the wealth and opportunities that slavery bought permeated across the whole of the British Isles, and can still be seen in our magnificent Georgian buildings, and street names such as Jamaica Street in Glasgow.

The history of the transatlantic slave trade is British history and Scotsmen and women played a strong part in its development as well as its abolition. These Scots, such as the slave trader and investor Richard Oswald, the abolitionist Lord Gardenstone, and the Glaswegian tobacco merchant John Glassford, are part of our history and that of slavery.

The exact figure for the number of West Africans captured and transported across the Atlantic is not known, but a conservative estimate is that **approximately 10 million West Africans were enslaved by Europeans over the whole period of the slave trade and approximately 10 million more perished during the process of capture and transportation.**

(Mimi Sheller, *Consuming the Caribbean: From Arawaks to Zombies* (London, 2003), 150. Adam Hochschild, *Bury the Chains: The British Struggle to Abolish Slavery* (London, 2005), 31)

The West Africans that were captured had their freedom removed and their own wishes ignored. Men, women and children were taken from their own countries and communities to be used as forced labour to create the wealth of the plantations. Children born to the enslaved were automatically enslaved themselves and could be sold away from their parents whenever their owner wished it. The enslaved were beaten, branded and abused, without access to the law.

The brutal transportation across the Atlantic, and the strict rules and punishments on the plantations, were used to control the enslaved, which resulted in many slaves dying during transportation or within the first year of reaching the plantation.

The severe treatment of the enslaved was carried out by ordinary British sailors, authorised by ships' captains and witnessed by ships' doctors. Scottish sailors took part in the slaving voyages, and Scottish ships' captains set out from ports in Scotland and from England on slave voyages. In addition Scottish merchants, such as Richard Oswald, were partners in slaving ventures in Scotland and the Americas and also in slave voyages that left from Liverpool, Bristol and London. Scottish merchants, including the Tobacco Lords of Glasgow, benefited from the sale of goods to West Africans and also the arrival of luxury goods from the Americas. Scottish investors, along with their English counterparts, benefited from all stages of the slave trade, including the preparations.

The plantations that the enslaved worked on were owned by European settlers. Many islands such as St Kitts and Jamaica, as well as the area of Virginia in mainland America, had Scottish owners and overseers. In Sierra Leone, West Africa, a hugely profitable private slaving fort was a London-Scottish venture. The fort, Bance Island, loaded on average 1,000 slaves a year on to ships from many countries.

In contrast the movement for the abolition of the slave trade created a model for political campaigning that still exists, and helped to introduce an era that championed the rights of the oppressed and fought the wealthy establishment. It was a grass roots movement encompassing thousands of people, many of whom campaigned tirelessly, despite not being entitled to the vote. It included ex-slaves such as Olaudah Equiano; social reformers such as Granville Sharpe; politicians such as William Wilberforce and passionate abolitionists such as Zachary Macauley. The abolition movement took nearly 40 years to reach its goal of ending the trade. However, it did not end slavery entirely: it took a further 30 years for all those people that were enslaved to be given their freedom.

During the years of British involvement in the slave trade millions of West Africans were sold to British owners and died serving them on the plantations. It was a system of forced unpaid labour that helped drive the British economy ahead of many of its rivals. British financial success from that time helped to develop the modern Britain that we live in today.

This discussion of Scotland and the Slave Trade, explores the following areas:

- The development of the slave trade
- The lives of the enslaved
- Legal cases before the abolition of the Slave Trade
- The abolition movement
- The Parliamentary process leading to abolition
- The turning of international opinion (1807 – 1838)
- The legacy for Scotland, Britain and the Caribbean

The *Triangular* Trade

75% of all Africa's exports in 18th century were enslaved humans –
at its height the slave trade removed

80,000

Africans per annum

Credit: The Branded Hand, c.1845 (daguerreotype) by Southworth, Albert
S. (1811-1894) & Hawes, Josiah (1808-1901) © Massachusetts Historical
Society, Boston, MA, USA / The Bridgeman Art Library
Nationality / copyright status: American / out of copyright

Chapter 2: The Triangular Trade

Trade Prior To the Development of the Transatlantic Slave Trade

From the early 16th century ships from Britain and Western Europe travelled to the African kingdoms to exchange goods from both sides. The West African people such as the Asante and Yoruba, and those from the Benin and Dahomy kingdoms were often skilled craftsmen whose expertise in gold and metal work was far more developed than the Europeans. The West Africans also produced other luxury goods, such as carved ivory. In 1700 the *African Merchant*, a Scottish Company Ship, returned from West Africa with a cargo that made nearly £4000 profit. In exchange for African goods the Europeans traded in cloth and raw metal materials, but as time went on they also traded in guns, fuelling local disputes and wars. The further step from trading goods to trading people was taken as the desire for profit was met by opportunity.

The Growth of Plantations and the Need for Labour

The climate and land on the Caribbean islands made the growing of some luxury crops such as sugar and tobacco possible. The colonisers pushed the native Indians off the land through force, enslavement, or as a result of the high death rate of the Indians from contracting European illnesses and disease. To make the maximum profit on the luxury goods, cheap hard working labour was needed to work with very labour intensive crops such as sugar and tobacco. In return for a free passage to the Americas, thousands of young men and women from Britain and Ireland signed contracts agreeing to work for an employer for 4 to 7 years as indentured labour. Indentured labour differed from slavery – the period of indenture was limited and the master owned the servant's time not the actual person.

Convicted criminals and political prisoners, including religious nonconformists, were also sent to the colonies as a workforce. In the late 17th century the religious turmoil in Scotland produced a regular supply of indentured labourers, whilst in England the Monmouth rebels were another source.[1] In 1651 Covenanters and Scottish royalists were amongst the 10,000 captured by Cromwell after battle, many of whom were sold as indentured labourers to the West Indies. In 1666 the city fathers of Edinburgh shipped off *"beggars, vagabonds and others not fitt to stay in the kingdome"* to Virginia in the *Phoenix of Leith* under Captain James Gibson. The Scots Privy Council also saw indentured labour as an opportunity to get rid of undesirables and those guilty of certain crimes, and they regularly sent people to Virginia as a punishment rather than keep them in jail.

Many of the labourers died on the journey or before their 4 to 7 years were complete due to the harsh conditions and the often brutal treatment by the plantation owners. Those that survived often remained in the Caribbean and became managers and overseers. Ultimately indentured labour did not bring the profit desired and a cheaper source of labour was still sought.

Formalising the trade

Europeans quickly realised the potential profit that could be made from buying and selling Africans, and plantation owners grasped the opportunity of using a malleable renewable labour force that did not require payment or recognition.

"Africans sold other Africans by choice because they stood to gain from it. Coercion and seduction took place. For centuries they practiced a trade between themselves that was similar to serfdom. Perhaps, when the Europeans arrived, they imagined that Atlantic slavery was just an extension of that system. But they couldn't have been more mistaken. The advent of white people introduced the ideology of race to slavery. Europe justified its brutality on the basis of its natural superiority to black people."

Mungo Park, a Scottish Doctor, 'Travels in the Interior Districts of Africa', 1799

Although the Portuguese had started the practice of transporting enslaved Africans to the

[1] On June 11 1685 the Duke of Monmouth landed at Lyme Regis in Dorset with the intention of removing King James II. The Duke was the illegitimate son of Charles II who had died 4 months earlier, James II was the younger brother of Charles II and the official legitimate heir, he was however also a Catholic. The Duke gathered the people up to fight for him as a Protestant and attacked the King's forces at the Battle of Sedgemoor, Bridgeport, Somerset July 6, 1685. The rebellion failed and the Duke was executed on July 15 1685.

plantations in the New World, the other West European countries quickly followed, with the British dominating the trade for years.

In 1562 Captain John Hawkins became the first British sailor to travel to West Africa, capture 300 African people, take them to the Americas (southern states of America and the islands of the Caribbean) and sell them as goods. With the money he made from selling people he bought luxury goods grown in the region from colonial plantation owners, and returned to Britain to continue his trading. Hawkins was part of a cycle that became known as the 'Triangular Trade' and at each of the three points of the triangle there was money to be made.

The Triangular Trade

The Triangular Trade started in Britain – the first stage was the journey to West Africa to exchange goods for captured Africans.

The second stage was the transportation of captured Africans across the Atlantic to the Americas to be sold as chattels, giving rise to the term 'chattel slavery'. This stage is commonly known as the Middle Passage.

The third stage was the return journey from the Americas with plantation-grown goods, bought from the profits of selling the Africans to the plantation owners. The goods that created such high profits included sugar, rum and tobacco.

Sugar was a very popular import into London and Bristol, which both had a boom in refineries and grocers. Scotland dominated the Virginian tobacco market.

The Royal African Company was formed to fully exploit and control the developing trade of enslaved people. The Royal African Company was issued with a Royal Charter in 1672. This gave it a monopoly in trading to Africa, including the slave trade. In the 1680s it was transporting approximately 5000 slaves per year. Between 1680 and 1688, it sponsored 249 voyages to Africa. However, the company was London based with mainly London businessmen benefiting. Merchant organisations from other cities such as Bristol and Liverpool lobbied to break the monopoly. Scottish merchants were also unhappy with the privileges of the company and took to organising illegal independent voyages. In 1695 the Company of Scotland Trading to Africa and the Indies was formed, with little success, due to the uncertainty of the trade and the risk of attack, although 1706 did see the success of the ship *Two Brothers of Leith*, which journeyed via Holland.

In 1698, the Royal African Company lost its monopoly and Bristol and Liverpool also officially became slaving ports. The 1707 Act of Union with England admitted Scotland into the general trade of the British Empire, although access to the African trade was still limited. Slave ships sailed out from the Clyde; how many is not known as the Port Books before 1742 did not survive. The Scottish enthusiasm for organising all aspects of the difficult three stage journey was patchy, many instead were content to invest in the voyages from the English ports for their slaving missions.

However, from the 1750s onwards ships did leave from Port Glasgow and Greenock for the triangular trade, often transporting enslaved Africans to Virginia as well as the Caribbean. After the American War of Independence the slave trade was consolidated into the ports of London and Liverpool, and Scottish investors and merchants invested through those routes. A steady direct trade was maintained with the Americas with the importing of slave-produced goods throughout the period and beyond.

There are dominant architectural reminders of Scotland's importance in the trading of sugar produced by enslaved labour, such as giant sugar warehouses in Greenock. Leading up to 1813 – 1814 one of the largest sugar companies in the world operated from Greenock. These warehouses signify the major role of Scottish plantation owners. By the early 19th century they owned a third of the plantations in Jamaica (which was the largest producer of sugar).

Capture and the Middle Passage

All along the West African coast, stretching across hundreds of miles, Europeans established trading networks and slave forts. The captured Africans were taken by other Africans to the forts or straight to the awaiting slaving vessels. Once captured, the Africans had their clothing removed and were put into chains. This was the start of the dehumanising process of turning individuals into objects and commodities. From then on they were considered enslaved and they had no idea what lay in store for them. Traders could spend up to six weeks gathering enough people to make the journey profitable before they eventually set out for the Caribbean.

"On that very day they made me a captive. They tore off my clothes, bound me with ropes, gave me a heavy load to carry. There they sold me to the Christians, and I was bought by a certain captain of a ship at that time. He sent me to a boat, and delivered me over to one of his sailors. The boat immediately pushed off, and I was carried on board of the ship. We continued on board ship, at sea, for three months, and then came on shore in the land of Jamaica. This was the beginning of my slavery until this day. I tasted the bitterness of slavery from them, and its oppressiveness!"

Abu-Bakr al-Siddiq of Timbuktu (b. 1790)

75% of all Africa's exports in the 18th century were enslaved humans – at its height the slave trade removed 80,000 Africans per annum.

(Adam Hochschild, *Bury the Chains: The British Struggle to Abolish the Slavery* (London, 2005), 2.)

The transportation across the Atlantic was extremely brutal and sometimes lasted three months. The mortality rate on the crossing was very high; figures taken from ships' logs and eyewitness accounts suggest that 1 in 4 people who left Africa died before they reached their destination. Conditions aboard the slave ships were appalling; huge numbers of people were crammed into very small spaces, people were packed like any other cargo and had little room to move or air to breathe. Head room was approximately 68cm with people packed on their sides. In 1788 the Dolben Act was passed by Parliament to restrict the number of enslaved transported according to the tonnage of the ship. However, the Act was regularly ignored.

Whilst on board the ship the Africans were at the mercy of the crew who regularly beat them to ensure subordination. Branding also took place and so did abuse of the women. The horrors of the Middle Passage were often used by the abolitionists to justify the ending of the trade.

How the money was made

At all sides of the triangle money could be made by merchants and business men in Britain. For example, Richard Oswald was born in Scotland, and he learnt his trade in Glasgow, Virginia and Jamaica. In 1746 he settled in London with his company, Grant, Oswald and Co. He owned ships, including slaving vessels, and his company owned Bance Island, one of the most famous and busiest slave forts, selling captured Africans. He owned shares in slave plantations in South Carolina, Jamaica and Florida. His ships carried the plantation-produced goods of sugar and tobacco back to Britain, where they were sold on. Oswald profited at every stage of the triangle.

He owned a 100,000 acre estate at Auchincruive in Scotland, and on his death he left a fortune of £500,000, equivalent to £40 million pounds today.

In Britain goods were specifically produced for the African market, and the slave ships were a lucrative source of money as they had to be specially adapted for carrying, men, women and children as cargo. Metal workers producing chains and shackles also benefited, as did insurers, investors and port authorities.

Alexander Horsburgh, the surgeon with responsibility for business affairs on the *Hannover*, noted in his journal (one of the earliest complete records of a slaving voyage) in

1720, that on his journey from the Clyde the goods they carried were made specifically for trade with West Africa. These goods included glass beads, cheap textiles, pewter ware, gunpowder, muskets, axes, cutlasses, brandy, rum and copper bars. Guns were also another profitable export, which in the long run helped to fuel the African wars that led to the availability of slaves. 150,000 per annum were exported to West Africa each year, from Birmingham alone.

In 1749 a male slave was bought at Elmina, now in present day Ghana, for 6 ounces of gold payable in equivalent goods. These were listed in the ledgers of the Dutch West India Company as follows:

2 muskets
40 pounds of gunpowder
1 anker brandy
1 piece cotton cloth
1 piece patterned Indian cloth
2 pieces gingham
2 iron rods
1 copper rod
4 pieces fine linen
1,000 beads
1 pewter basin
20 pounds cowrie shells

Merchants in Britain benefited from the investors who bought their goods to take out, or alternatively merchants received their share of payment once the slaving vessel returned from the Caribbean.

Profits varied from trip to trip, depending on the number of captured Africans that died during transportation. Encountering pirates or bad weather also affected the potential financial profit made by each ship.

One journey for which the profit was recorded was that of the *Molly*. The *Molly* left Bristol for West Africa in January 1751, leaving with 155 Africans on board. It arrived in Jamaica in December 1751 with 125 Africans still alive for sale. The *Molly* arrived back in Britain in May 1752. The total investment was £3,864.17.1, of which £2,333.13.4 constituted trade goods. The sale of slaves at Jamaica was conducted by Bright, Hall & Co, including 49 men, 32 women, 20 boys and 24 girls. The average price was £28.20 sterling. Profits on the voyage came to £2,570.63

Who Owned the Plantations and Ran the Colonies?

The British Islands of the Caribbean and the colonies of the Americas were owned and run by British settlers and administrators. It was common for merchants in Britain to establish their own plantations or create relationships with agreed suppliers for plantation goods. Therefore

it was British people who bought, sold, and oversaw the enslaved. Networks or communities were often established that resulted from ties back home. Alexander Horsburgh, the surgeon with responsibility for business affairs on the *Hannover*, noted in his journal in 1720, that there was an established Scottish network in Barbados, Antigua and St Kitts. The *Hannover* sailed from Port Glasgow and Horsburgh was instructed by its Scottish owners which Scottish plantation owners to contact with his cargo of enslaved Africans. These included Colonel William McDowall of Wigtonshire, a plantation owner on St Kitts.

Lady Nugent, the wife of the one time Governor of Jamaica, also noted the high presence of the

Scotsmen on the islands. That Scottish presence started in the early years of the colonies and continued. Mrs Alison Blyth noted on her visit to Jamaica in 1826 that:

"...the Lord indeed knoweth. I always thought that wherever I went I would be proud of my country but here I feel almost ashamed to say I am a native of Scotland, when I see how her sons have degenerated".

The colonies were an important military base. A number of Scottish regiments were sent to the islands, especially at times of rebellion. From 1793 to 1798 and from 1800 to 1803 the esteemed officer Sir Thomas Makdougall Brisbane of Ayrshire served in the islands, commanding at one point the 69th regiment.

Scotland and Virginian tobacco

The Virginian colony, Chesapeake, was Britain's first permanent settlement in North America and was founded in 1607[2]. The colony became popular with people leaving Britain to find success overseas. Many Scots who left Scotland as indentured labour ended up on the colony and as a result a strong network built up there. Virginia became the centre for tobacco, a high intensity crop dependent on enslaved labour. Due to the Scottish connections and the easy route from Scotland to Virginia, Glasgow became the centre for tobacco imports into Britain. By 1720 Glasgow imported over half of all the American slave-grown tobacco.

Glasgow merchants often owned the plantations in Virginia growing the crops, thus making them the owners of enslaved Africans on whose labour they became extremely wealthy. Merchants such as Andrew Buchanan, James Dunlop, John Glassford and James Wilson built grand houses in Glasgow, and the surrounding streets are still named after them. The business of importing and refinement of tobacco resulted in the Glasgow population expanding to over 70,000 by 1804, and also in the decision to expand Glasgow itself as a port rather than relying on Port Glasgow further down the Clyde.

[2] Chesapeake was officially an English colony, although many Scots and Irish Scots were known to have settled and owned land there.

TheLives of the
Enslaved

"*All…slaves…shall be held to be real estate. If any slave resist his master…correcting such slave, and shall happen to be killed on such correction…the master shall be free of all punishment.*"

1705 Virginian General Assembly

Credit: Slaves from Africa packed on the deck of a slaver ship bound for America (engraving) by American School © Private Collection/ Peter Newark American Pictures / The Bridgeman Art Library
Nationality / copyright status: American / out of copyright

Chapter 3: The Lives of the Enslaved

Slave Auctions

After spending weeks on a ship, the enslaved that arrived in the Americas were usually sold by auction, unless an agreement had been made earlier. Slave auctions were advertised and plantation owners or their agents would always try to get the best price. The enslaved would be inspected whilst naked. To get the best price slave traders would rub palm oil into the enslaved's skin to make it shine and dye their hair to cover grey.

Once the sale had taken place the enslaved could be branded with their new owner's sign. They would also be renamed with a European name or a random word, anything to try and remove the identity of the enslaved and push them further into submission. To add to the humiliation it was unlikely that the enslaved person understood what was being said to them. They might also be sold separately from any friends or family, including children, and put to work on a plantation where no-one spoke their language or came from their part of Africa. Slave auctions were also held for those already enslaved on the islands.

Mary Prince was born into slavery in Bermuda in 1788. The following recollection is of her mother being ordered to take her and her sisters to the auction, and is taken from her narrative, recorded and dictated by herself after running away from her owners and reaching London in 1828:

"With my sisters we reached Hamble Town about four o'clock in the afternoon. We followed mother to the market-place, where she placed us in a row against a large house, with our backs to the wall and our arms folded in front. I stood first, Hannah next to me, then Dinah; and our mother stood beside us, crying. My heart throbbed with grief and terror so violently that I pressed my hands tightly across my breast, but I couldn't keep it still, and it continued to leap as though it would burst out of my body. But who cared for that? Did any of the bystanders think of the pain that wrung the hearts of the negro woman and her young ones? No, no! They weren't all bad, I dare say, but slavery hardens white people's hearts towards the blacks.

"At length the auctioneer arrived and asked my mother which was the eldest. She pointed to me. He took me by the hand, and led me out into the middle of the street. I was soon surrounded by strange men, who examined and handled me like a butcher with a calf or a lamb he was about to purchase, and who talked about my shape and size as if I couldn't understand what they were saying. I was then put up to sale. The bidding commenced at a few pounds, and gradually rose to fifty-seven. People said that I'd fetched a great sum for so young a slave.

"I then saw my sisters sold to different owners. When the sale was over, my mother hugged and kissed us, and mourned over us, begging us to keep a good heart, and do our duty to our new masters. It was a sad parting; one went one way, one another, and our poor mammy went home with nothing."

Daily Life

The plantation owners devised strict codes for keeping the enslaved separate and for justifying the brutality that was meted out to them. The enslaved could be kept permanently shackled, and beatings and floggings were daily occurrences, for the slightest hint of resistance or simply as a warning to others.

The majority of the enslaved men and women were sold as field slaves, irrespective of what skills they may have used in Africa. They worked all day, sometimes for 16 or 18 hours if it was harvest time, carrying out back breaking work in the hot and humid climate. They lived in basic huts and were provided with some food and clothing and sometimes a little patch of land to grow additional food. The enslaved were given Sundays off, but it was initially forbidden to convert them to Christianity or teach them to read or write, which would threaten the perceived concept that the Africans were "heathens" and "stupid". Later the arrival of non-conformist missionaries challenged those rules. The majority of the enslaved lived short lives[3], worked until exhaustion or death as they were seen as being easily replaced.

---

[3] It was unusual for an enslaved African to live beyond their forties in the Caribbean. Many did not live beyond their twenties depending on their age on arrival.

Resistance and Escape

John Newton[4], a slave ship captain who later turned to evangelical Christianity and spoke against the slave trade, said that at least 1 in 10 slaving ships experienced an uprising.

"On Tuesday the 18th of last October, happened a most melancholy and unhappy circumstance in the Road of Mouri belonging to the Dutch settlement, where was riding at anchor a Dutch ship full of slaves almost ready to take her departure from the coast. But the ill treatment of the unfeeling Captain incensed the poor captives so highly that they rose upon the ship's crew in his absence and took possession of the vessel. They consisted in number about 150. But the most dreadful circumstance of all is that after having laid their scheme with subtlety and art, and decoying as many of their countrymen who came far and near to plunder on board and near the ship, and also some white sailors from an English ship in hopes of relieving them, were all indiscriminately blown up to upwards of three or four hundred souls. This revengeful but very rash proceeding we are here made to understand to be entirely owning to the Captain's brutish behaviour, who did not allow even his own sailors, much more the slaves, a sufficient maintenance to support nature. If this is really the case, can we but help figuring to ourselves the true picture of inhumanity those unhappy creatures suffer in their miserable state of bondage, under the different degrees of austere masters they unfortunately fall in with, in the West Indies?"
Philip Quaque, Cape Coast Castle, February 8th, 1786

On the plantation resistance took many forms. Spiritual and personal resistance were the strongest. The enslaved created new communities, sharing and preserving customs, and in the little free time that they had they made clothes, cooking utensils and basic musical instruments. Many had grown up in the tradition of oral histories and they continued that tradition – telling the stories from their ancestors and repeating the traditions of their homeland.

[4] He is also well-known as the author of the hymn *Amazing Grace*.

Amongst themselves they continued to use their original names and named their children according to the customs they had left behind.

Despite the risk there was also physical resistance through escape. Escape often depended on the geography of the island – was there anywhere to run to? On the smaller islands this was difficult but on the larger islands such as Jamaica there were groups of ex-slaves who lived in the mountains. Runaway notices were often to be seen on the islands, with severe punishments for those who were recaptured. In some instances those recaptured would have a foot cut off to stop them from doing it again and as a warning to others; some would even die as a result of their punishments.

"All…slaves…shall be held to be real estate. If any slave resist his master…correcting such slave, and shall happen to be killed on such correction…the master shall be free of all punishment."
1705 Virginian General Assembly

Over the years resistance in its many forms grew. Some plantation owners responded by giving greater freedoms to the enslaved. Others, however, introduced yet harsher methods of repression, but it did not stop the rebellions.

The Enslaved Who Lived In Scotland

The vast majority of enslaved Africans were taken from West Africa to the Americas for work on the plantations. However, a number of white masters brought the enslaved with them when they visited or returned to Britain. Family portraits including enslaved Africans are found in Scotland. The painting of the Glassford family in the People's Palace, Glasgow, from about 1760, seems to have had the presence of an African enslaved servant 'painted out' at a later date.

The exact number of enslaved Africans in Britain is not known, but records such as runaway slave notices and church records provide some information. There are 70 records of enslaved Africans in Scotland in the 18th century.

Portrait of John Glassford of Dougalston at home with his family in the Shawfield Mansion. An African servant originally stood in the gap on the left but may have been removed from the painting later. Image courtesy of Glasgow Museums and Art Galleries.

Legal Cases

before the abolition of the Slave Trade

The practice of owning people did not become common in Britain and as a result a number of contradictory legal decisions had been made that raised the question of the rights of the enslaved, as well as the legal right to own people in Britain. The outcomes of these cases also influenced the abolition movement.

Credit: Abolition of Colonial Slavery Meeting, 1830 (letterpress) by English School, (19th century) © Private Collection / The Bridgeman Art Library Nationality / copyright status: English / out of copyright

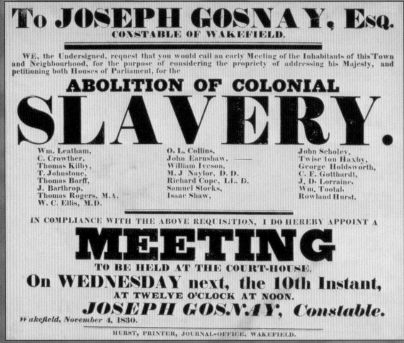

To JOSEPH GOSNAY, Esq.
CONSTABLE OF WAKEFIELD.

WE, the Undersigned, request that you would call an early Meeting of the Inhabitants of this Town and Neighbourhood, for the purpose of considering the propriety of addressing his Majesty, and petitioning both Houses of Parliament, for the

ABOLITION OF COLONIAL
SLAVERY.

Wm. Leatham,	O. L. Collins,	John Scholey,
C. Crowther,	John Earnshaw, ——	Twise ton Haxby,
Thomas Kilby,	William Iveson,	George Holdsworth,
T. Johnstone,	M. J Naylor, D. D.	C. F. Gotthardt,
Thomas Barff,	Richard Cope, LL. D.	J. D. Lorraine,
J. Barthrop,	Samuel Stocks,	Wm. Tootal,
Thomas Rogers, M.A.	Isaac Shaw,	Rowland Hurst.
W. C. Ellis, M.D.		

IN COMPLIANCE WITH THE ABOVE REQUISITION, I DO HEREBY APPOINT A
MEETING
TO BE HELD AT THE COURT-HOUSE,
On WEDNESDAY next, the 10th Instant,
AT TWELVE O'CLOCK AT NOON.
JOSEPH GOSNAY, Constable.
Wakefield, November 4, 1830.

HURST, PRINTER, JOURNAL-OFFICE, WAKEFIELD.

Chapter 4: Legal Cases Before the Abolition of the Slave Trade

James Montgomery

James Montgomery, an enslaved African, was brought from Virginia to Ayrshire by Robert Sheddan. Sheddan wanted Montgomery, then called 'Shanker', apprenticed to a joiner so that he would learn a skill and could then be sold for a large profit back in Virginia. When 'Shanker' decided to be baptised in Beith Parish Church with the name James Montgomery in April 1756, Sheddan objected. Montgomery was dragged to Port Glasgow behind horses to be taken back to Virginia but he escaped to Edinburgh before the ship sailed. Montgomery sought justice but before a decision could be made by judges he died in Tolbooth Gaol.

David Spens

David Spens was known as 'Black Tom' until he was baptised in Wemyss Parish Church in September 1769. Spens was an enslaved African brought from the Home estates in Grenada to Methil in Fife by Dr David Dalrymple. After he was baptised Spens returned to his master stating *"I am now by the Christian Religion liberate and set at freedom from my yoke, bondage, and slavery"*. He was shielded in his declaration by a local farmer, John Henderson. Spens threatened legal action against Dalrymple if he tried to *"deprive the sovereign Lord the King of a good subject"*. Spens was immediately arrested, but with the assistance of several local lawyers he was able to issue writs for wrongful arrest. The local churches and the miners and salters of West Fife collected funds for his assistance. Spens was released from jail but Dalrymple died before the Court of Session decided the case.

James Somerset

When Charles Stewart travelled from Boston, America, to Britain he brought the enslaved James Somerset with him. In 1771 Somerset ran away from Stewart but was recaptured and imprisoned on a ship that was to sail to Jamaica, where he was to be sold. Three people witnessed the recapture and reported it to the Lord Chief Justice and he ordered that Somerset was to be kept in the country until a case could be heard. The case was heard in 1772. Granville Sharp, the abolitionist campaigner, assisted Somerset with legal support. Sharp argued that no man at that time was or could be a slave in England and that the laws of the American colonies had no force in Britain. Against Somerset's lawyers was the opinion of sections of the trading community that feared that if all slaves in British ports were set free thousands of pounds would be lost. The Lord Chief Justice made a carefully worded statement: *In England no master was allowed to take a slave by force to be sold abroad because he had deserted his service or for any other reason whatever.*

The ruling was interpreted by many as meaning that slaves in Britain were free. That was not the case, but after it was made many slaves deserted their owners anyway and the case provided a pivotal decision that affected attitudes and lives.

Joseph Knight

Mansfield's judgment was seen by Joseph Knight, an enslaved African from the Americas living in Perthshire with his 'owner' Sir John Wedderburn[5]. Knight demanded wages for his work and to be able to leave Wedderburn after seeing the judgment. He ran away when this was refused and Wedderburn had him arrested. The case was taken to court and a number of key opponents of slavery came to Knight's defence. James Boswell and Samuel Johnson supported Knight and helped in his representation when the court case was heard at Perth and then on appeal at the Court of Session in Edinburgh in 1778. Both courts came to the same conclusion that the law of

[5] John Wedderburn and his brother James were Scottish Plantation owners and slave dealers. Inveresk Lodge was bought by James Wedderburn with some of the fortune he made in Jamaica. His mixed-race son, Robert Wedderburn, was born a slave and was a well-known anti-slavery abolitionist in London in the later 18th and early 19th centuries. He published the pamphlet *Horrors of Slavery*.

Scotland did not allow slavery. Lord Auchenleck (father of James Boswell) stated *"although in the plantations they have laid hold poor blacks and made slaves of them, yet I do not think that is agreeable to humanity, not to say to the Christian religion"*. This Scottish judgment on slavery went further than the English Somerset case.

Case of the *Zong*

The slave ship the *Zong* left the coast of Africa in September 1781. Far more enslaved Africans had been packed onto the ship than the hold was adapted for and disease spread quickly, exacerbated by malnutrition. By November 1781, 60 Africans had died. The Captain, Luke Collingwood, decided to throw the remaining 131 Africans overboard to stop the disease.

Under British law if the cargo, in this case people, was lost it would be underwritten by the insurers. If, however, the sick Africans failed to be sold in the Caribbean then the fault and loss would be the crew's. The claim by the Captain to the insurers was that there was not enough water for those on board. That claim was found to be false as 430 gallons of water were on board when the *Zong* reached port. In 1783 the case went to court, not over the death of the Africans but as an insurance dispute. The British courts ruled that the ship owners could not claim insurance on the loss of the Africans, however no officers or crew were charged with or prosecuted for murder.

The case received a lot of attention in the press and was used by abolitionists to highlight the horrendous way in which the enslaved were transported across the Atlantic and the status given to their lives.

Abolition
begins

"The African slave trade in its present mode of existence and throughout all stages" was *"a direct violation of all Jehovah's righteous laws that positively require every man to love his neighbour as himself."*

Credit: The Great Anti-Slavery Meeting of 1841, at Exeter Hall, engraved by Henry Melville (fl.1826-41) (engraving) by Shepherd, Thomas Hosmer (1792-1864) (after) © Guildhall Library, City of London / The Bridgeman Art LibraryNationality / copyright status: English / out of copyright

Chapter 5: Abolition Begins

Supporting the Trade

The argument for the trade was primarily based on the economic advantages of both the trade and the production of crops that yielded high profits due to forced unpaid labour. In the early years there were those that justified the trade on the grounds that the Africans were inferior to Europeans, and that prejudice continued even amongst some of those who opposed slavery. David Hume's view was:

"I am apt to suspect the Negroes to be naturally inferior to the Whites. There scarcely ever was a civilised nation of that complexion, nor even any individual, eminent either in action or in speculation. No ingenious manufacture among them, no arts, no sciences."

The Kirkliston born Archibald Dalzel, former Governor of Cape Coast Castle in modern day Ghana, argued that slavery was a 'civilising process' which 'rescued Africans'. However, the conversion of the enslaved to Christianity meant they were perceived to be at least equal in the eyes of God. The main thrust of the pro-slavery debate therefore remained about economic advantage and disputing the abolitionists' arguments that the trade was cruel.

"The slave trade has been the source and chief foundation of the riches, strength, power and greatness of this kingdom. There is no branch of any foreign trade whatsoever, beyond the limits of Europe, so naturally adapted to the interests of Britain and her plantations, as the Trade to Africa."
Charles Davenant, Reflections on the Constitution and Management of the Trade to Africa (1709)

The Case for Abolition

There had always been people who objected to the slave trade and slavery, but the details of the slave trade were not known amongst the general public. There were few newspapers at this time, so information was mainly from sailors returning home. However, details could be attributed to individual voyages as opposed to overall trends. The Abolitionists brought slavery to the attention of the general public. However, in the last quarter of the 18th century, when the slave trade was at its peak, a number of factors came together that forced British people to consider their country's involvement in the system. The new non-conformist religion questioned the slave trade on moral grounds at the same time as the enlightenment was raising the issue of the rights of man and the treatment of others.

Frances Hutcheson in Glasgow and Adam Ferguson from Edinburgh produced strong theological and humanitarian arguments against slavery, whilst Adam Smith wrote his position of opposition from a secular perspective. Concurrently the lecturer James Beattie was ensuring that his students at Aberdeen University were fully aware of the horrors of the trade.

In addition the continued resistance of the enslaved people themselves was having an impact on those involved in slavery and living in the Caribbean. The process of change took a huge cultural shift in Britain, and it also meant a shift in the machinery of government as the slave trade and slavery had become rooted in both the legal system and the economic foundations of the Empire.

In 1787 the Society for the Abolition of the Slave Trade was formed in London. It was led by Quakers but also appealed to others, such as key abolitionists Thomas Clarkson and Granville Sharp. The society decided to focus on the Parliamentary campaign, and the initial aim was to collect information and evidence that could be presented to Parliament to win over MPs. It was decided to focus on ending the trade rather than slavery itself. This was deemed more achievable, whereas to demand an end to slavery would be seen to be threatening people's property, which is what the enslaved were considered to be at that time.

As well as campaigning in Parliament the society encouraged the setting up of local and regional abolition committees. Those committees encouraged a number of activities, including the refusal to buy slave-produced sugar, significant at a time when in 1800 British families spent 6% of the household expenditure per annum on sugar. The Abolitionist Committee in Edinburgh, led by Francis, Lord Gardenstone, was thought to be the third strongest in Britain after those of London and Manchester.

A main focus of the campaign and of the abolitionist pamphlets was the horrors of the Middle Passage. Many surgeons or sailors were called upon to give evidence of what they had witnessed on the Atlantic crossing.

Thomas Smith of Arbroath gave evidence to the agents of William Wilberforce. Thomas was 20 years old when he left his home in 1762. He was recruited by David Adam, the Scottish master of the slaving ship the *Anne* of London, of which nearly a quarter of the crew were Scottish. Disaster hit the *Anne* after it reached West Africa and Thomas, stranded, signed onto the Liverpool slaving vessel the *Squirrel*. He reported that the deliberate brutalisation of the slaves started the moment they came on board.

All the males were forcibly circumcised, branded with a hot iron and loaded down with heavy shackles. Completely naked, they were chained together in tens by the neck, hands and feet, bound down with irons so that their hands/limbs were crushed, almost unto death, and all for the purpose of maintaining due subordination, as it was called, and preserving the peace and safety of everyone onboard. They were not unchained during the entire Atlantic journey, everything would be conducted as a group. If any died during the night their bodies were thrown overboard and the survivors were forced to watch the sharks eat the body. Women and children along with the men were regularly flogged to ensure their compliance. Anyone refusing to eat was flogged. Smith was also horrified by the treatment of the female slaves who were subjected *"to the wanton and unrestrained licentiousness of the crew"*. Of the 450 onboard 45 died during the journey from their treatment and from disease spread due to the severity of their conditions on the ship. Smith left the ship in Jamaica horrified by his experiences.

James Ramsey had been a surgeon in the Navy and he had lived on St Kitts. The abolitionist MP Sir Charles Middleton asked Ramsey to give evidence to the Parliamentary enquiry into the trade. As well as being repulsed by slavery he was also disgusted by the slave trade's disregard for the life of sailors. He wanted a scheme to promote fisheries in North East Scotland, where he had come from, and to open up proper trade with Africa. He argued that *"Instead of this our chief aim in our trade to that continent is the commerce of slaves which destroys our seamen annually by thousands"*. The plight of the sailors on slave ships also became a key tool in the abolitionist argument against the trade.

The image of the *Brookes Ship* became a famous piece of abolitionist propaganda, used to show how the captured Africans were packed into the ships hold as cargo with little or no room to move. In reality the *Brookes Ship* shown in the image holding 454 people stacked in rows had actually carried 609 people in previous voyages.

Leading Abolitionists

Olaudah Equiano (1745 – 1797)

Olaudah Equiano, also called Gustavus Vassa, was a former slave who wrote about his experiences and toured with his book as part of the abolitionist movement. When he was 11 years old he was sold to a captain in the Royal Navy, Michael Pascal, who gave him the name

Credit: Olaudah Equiano alias Gustavus Vassa, a slave, 1789 (mezzotint)
© British Library, London, UK / © British Library Board. All Rights Reserved / The Bridgeman Art Library Nationality / copyright status: out of copyright

Gustavus Vassa. Later he was sold to Robert King, a Quaker merchant in Philadelphia. King converted him to Christianity and taught him to read and write. At the age of 21 years Equiano was able to buy his freedom and he became a seaman, travelling over the world. He eventually settled in London and became involved with the abolitionist movement. In 1789 he wrote *"The Interesting Narrative of the Life of Olaudah Equiano, or Gustavus Vassa the African"*. The book made him famous and furthered the abolitionist cause. He travelled extensively across the British Isles selling and reading from his book. In 1792 he married and shortly afterwards he set off on his Scottish tour to talk to audiences in the region, including Edinburgh, Glasgow, Paisley, Dundee, Perth and Aberdeen. Later, in 1792, Equiano became involved in regular correspondence in the Glasgow Courier over the issue of abolition.

Ignatius Sanchos (1729 – 1780)

Ignatius Sanchos was born in 1729 on a slave ship in the mid-Atlantic. His mother died soon afterwards, and his father killed himself rather than be enslaved. In 1731 Ignatius was brought to England and forced to live with three sisters in Greenwich. They did not believe in educating him; nonetheless, Ignatius taught himself to read and write. Eventually, he ran away and stayed with the Duke of Montagu, who lived in nearby Blackheath. Sanchos worked as a butler, but also wrote poetry and two stage plays. He composed music, with three collections of songs, minuets, and other pieces for various instruments all published

anonymously. In 1773, he left the service of the Montagus and opened a grocery shop in Charles Street, Westminster, with his wife Anne. Sanchos frequently wrote about his experiences as an African in Britain, once describing himself as only a lodger and hardly that. He died in 1780. Two years later his Letters were published and were an immediate best-seller, attracting over 1,200 subscribers.

William Wilberforce (1759 – 1833)

Wilberforce was born in Hull to a wealthy merchant family. After university he became an MP for the town and also converted to evangelical Christianity. He became interested in social reform and became involved with abolitionists. He initially only believed in ending

Credit: Portrait of William Wilberforce (1759-1833) 1828 (oil on canvas) (see 112022) by Lawrence, Sir Thomas (1769-1830) © National Portrait Gallery, London, UK / The Bridgeman Art Library Nationality / copyright status: English / out of copyright

the slave trade not slavery itself. He was extremely influential as a speaker and was a key member of the group that influenced others both inside and outside Parliament to join the cause. As an MP he was able to introduce bills to Parliament to abolish the trade. After 1807 he became concerned with the terrible conditions the enslaved continued to live in and he supported the complete abolition of slavery. He died 3 days after the bill to abolish slavery was passed in 1833.

Robert Burns (1759 – 1796)

Robert Burns, the celebrated Scottish poet, was born into humble beginnings. In 1783 he was almost penniless and decided to accept an offer to go to Jamaica as a bookkeeper on an estate. To raise the fare to get from Greenock to Jamaica on the *Nancy* he was persuaded to raise a subscription to publish some of his poems. The publication and success of the Kilmarnock edition changed his mind about leaving.

He became affected by the abolitionist cause. The circles he mixed in, especially after the publication of his first book of poetry, would have opened him to abolitionist messages. A number of writers refer to Burns' personal dislike of anyone being treated in a servile manner, and his interest in social injustice issues. In 1792 he published 'The Slave's Lament', based on the stories he heard coming from the Scottish estates in Virginia (see inside back cover for text).

Zachary Macauley (1768 – 1838)

Zachary Macauley, from Argyll, went to Jamaica in 1784 as a book keeper or overseer on a sugar plantation. Initially he was appalled at the conditions meted out to the enslaved, but eventually became, as he described it, "callous and indifferent". He returned to Britain in 1789 and visited his sister who had married Thomas Babington, a close friend of William Wilberforce. There he became a convert to the abolitionist cause and in 1790 he went to Sierra Leone, the settlement established for ex-slaves in West

[6] Sierra Leone was first settled by freed slaves sent from England and Canada in 1787. Later the Sierra Leone Company was founded and the idea was to have an area settled by freed and ex-slaves. The idea was supported by the abolitionist Granville Sharpe. The plan was not very successful as many of the Black settlers died, however in 1808 Freetown in Sierra Leone became a British colony and enslaved Africans captured by the British Navy on Slave Ships were often released to that colony.

Africa[6]. He became Governor of the colony in 1794. Living in an area surrounded by hostile slave ships further convinced Macauley of the need to end the trade. He collected evidence for the London committee by travelling on a slave ship to the West Indies whilst on home leave in 1795. He recorded his thoughts and findings in classical Greek to keep them secret from the crew.

His major contribution was to work on the collection and collating of the huge volume of evidence and drafting of reports. In the 1820s he campaigned tirelessly for the total abolition of slavery and went on to establish the Anti-Slavery Society in 1823 and edit the Anti-Slavery Monthly Reporter.

Thomas Clarkson (1760 – 1846)

The Reverend Thomas Clarkson was a leading abolition campaigner. He collected information about the horror and injustice of the slave trade, which would convince people to support its abolition. He rode around the country on horseback for two years, interviewing 20,000 sailors and obtaining equipment used on slave ships.

Clarkson was often in danger when he visited ports like Liverpool and Bristol where there were economic interests in continuing the slave trade. In Bristol, he interviewed sailors and discovered a lot about the poor conditions and abuse that European sailors as well as enslaved Africans had to endure on these voyages.

Credit: Reverend Thomas Clarkson, M.A. (1760-1846) engraved by John Young (1755-1825) 1789 (engraving) by Breda. Carl Frederik van (1759-1818) (after) © Guildhall Art Gallery, City of London / The Bridgeman Art Library Nationality / copyright status: Swedish / out of copyright

Thomas Clarkson collected objects which he used in campaigning lectures against the slave trade. The items were kept in a chest equipped with trays and boxes. There were objects that display the skill and talent of African craftspeople, such as dyed cloth. There were also samples of natural products such African ivory, gum, rice, two kinds of pepper and rare and beautiful woods.

Clarkson carried his 'collection of African productions' everywhere to prove that Britain could carry on a profitable trade with Africa without slavery or the slave trade. Clarkson's arguments for trading with Africa had a major impact on the later European explorers and anti-slavery campaigners in Africa, like David Livingstone.

William Dickson (published work 1789 – 1815)

William Dickson of Moffat, Dumfriesshire, was the Secretary to the Governor of Barbados from 1783 to 1786. Whilst there he became very opposed to slavery and on his return in 1789 he wrote the book 'Letters on Slavery'. His book was considered too radical by those focusing on ending only the trade but Thomas Clarkson saw Dickson's value and sent him to Scotland to gather support for the end of the trade.

During the early months of 1792 Dickson travelled around Scotland presenting evidence to church groups and meeting with local committees to raise their awareness. It was on his instigation that Scotland became a hotbed of petition-signing. Due to his endeavours in Scotland Dickson was awarded an honorary doctorate by Aberdeen University.

As well as raising awareness Dickson also collected evidence from people about the trade.

"Mr McNeill mentioned…a Scotsman in Jamaica…who when his slaves were worn out and judged by the Doctor on the estate to be capable of no more work, had them carried to what he called the 'launch' which consisted of a few boards whose ends inclined over a great precipice and from thence he had them launched into eternity."

(Adam Hochschild, *Bury the Chains: The British Struggle to Abolish Slavery* (London, 2005), 227)

The Grass Roots and Women

Success depended on mobilising public opinion on a scale never seen before in Britain. The techniques used by the abolitionists laid the ground for modern campaigning.

Pamphlets describing the horrors of slavery and life for the enslaved were published. Poetry was also used as a way to spread the message. All levels of society were involved, but only men could sign petitions, and furthermore, only a privileged few of those could vote. Women and children expressed their support by reading abolitionist literature and singing abolitionist songs. Rallies, or public readings of abolitionist pamphlets were a popular and successful way of spreading the message.

Women wore jewellery that advertised their support for abolition and wrote poetry. Women also usually managed household spending and chose not to buy goods produced by enslaved people.

The efforts of women are all the more remarkable because at the time they had very few rights of their own and were considered the property of their husbands or fathers. This explains why so little is known about who they were. After 1807, 73 female Anti Slavery Societies were established across Britain. The Quakers Jane Smeal, from Glasgow, and Eliza Wigham, from Edinburgh, were key in helping to lead the way. These groups were the first to demand the immediate emancipation of the enslaved, and both these women went on to be involved with other human rights and emancipation work.

The Wedgwood pottery company played an important role in the Abolition movement through its owner Thomas Wedgwood. He commissioned and had designed and made ornamental goods and pottery bearing the logo of the kneeling enslaved African with the statement 'Am I not a Man, Am I not a Brother'.

Petitions

In the 18th century very few men were permitted to vote in Britain, less than half a million people in a population of over 20 million. The most popular and important way for people to express their opinions, therefore, was through the signing of petitions that were presented to Parliament. Between 1787 – 1792 approximately 13% of the adult male population signed a petition against the slave trade. The quotation below reflects the extent of the petition movement and the cynicism with which it was viewed by some:

"Petitions have been pouring in from every part of the Island, and a great number indeed from Scotland, some of them from the Highland Parishes where the Fools who sign the petitions at the Black Smith's shop, which is the Country Coffee House, never saw the Face of a Black, and there is not one of the parishes from whence there are not some of the better farmer's Sons sent to the West Indies and employed in the different plantations as overseers."

General James Grant of Ballindalloch, Banff (Governor of East Florida) to Lord Cornwallis, 22 April 1792, PRO 30/11/270, fo. 95

In Edinburgh in 1792, at a massive public meeting supporting abolition, 3,685 men signed a petition on the spot. When unrolled the petition stretched the entire length of the House of Commons floor. In Glasgow a further 13,000 signed. That year Scotland sent 185 petitions out of a British and Irish total of 519.

Scottish Churches

The Scottish churches and theologians were some of the main drivers of the abolition movement in Scotland. As in England and elsewhere the argument about justification of the trade through biblical quotations was under dispute. The quotation below is an extract from the Glasgow Courier in March 1792, where a series of letters began to explore and argue for and against the trade and slavery. The opponent of slavery quoted called himself 'A Friend of Mankind', and disputed the use of a Biblical quotation.

"And ye shall take them…to inherit them for a possession, they shall be your bond-men for ever" THUS SAITH THE LORD! The Slave Trade is founded in cruelty and injustice. THUS SAITH THE Presbytery of Glasgow."

The 'Friend' argued, along with James Ramsey of Fraserburgh, a former ship's surgeon, that the conditions of the capture and experiences of the Middle Passage differentiated the trade from that of slavery in the Bible. William Robertson the historian argued simply that the trade stood against *"the spirit and genius of the Christian Religion"*.

Various groups from the Christian church spoke out against the trade from their pulpits, with a number also publishing theological pamphlets against the trade. Divine vengeance was a common theme, and was often used in the petitions of 1788 and 1792. One minister from Dundee wrote a poem on the theme of divine vengeance on those who took part in the trade to spread the cause. John Erskine, Scotland's leading evangelical, and the Reverend Robert Balfour of Glasgow argued that the trade was damaging to the missionary activities in Africa.

The Relief Presbytery of Hamilton declined to petition but did declare *"the African slave trade in its present mode of existence and throughout all stages"* was *"a direct violation of all Jehovah's righteous laws that positively require every man to love his neighbour as himself"* which had a huge impact on many followers.

Although the Church was a key driver in the Abolitionist movement, the Church of Scotland did not petition Parliament to end the Slave Trade or Slavery.

37

Parliamentary
Process

Timeline of Parliamentary Activity

1787: The Middle Passage Act

1788: 103 petitions are handed into Parliament.

1792: 310 petitions are handed into Parliament, the greatest number submitted about one subject, totalling over 400,000 names. The debate rages.

1776: David Hartley proposes the first bill to the House of Commons – that the Slave Trade is contrary to the laws of God and the rights of man. It is defeated.

1790: William Wilberforce presents the first abolition Bill to the House of Commons, but it does not pass.

1792: House of Commons votes in favour of the abolition of the trade but the Bill is rejected by the House of Lords.

1807: The Bill is passed in February and becomes law on 25 March.

Chapter 6: Parliamentary Process

The Parliamentary process leading to abolition was a difficult one. Many of those who sat in both the House of Commons and the House of Lords had connections to some aspect of the Triangular Trade. Even if they had no direct relationship, as men of power and wealth they usually had other business interests that required the British economy to be successful. It was no great surprise that the first bill introduced in 1776 to abolish the trade failed.

John Anderson, the nephew of Richard Oswald, the Scottish merchant and slave trader, sat in Parliament as an MP. John Anderson had inherited part of his uncle's empire, and had also been a slave ship captain. He was determined to continue with the practice of the trade. He spoke out against abolition and voted to keep the trade alongside MPs representing Liverpool.

The fight was difficult, with many influential people from across Britain writing and campaigning on the issue. The events of the French revolution frightened some politicians out of challenging the status quo. However after much lobbying the tide began to turn.

In 1792, after receiving 519 petitions, Parliament debated whether to abolish the Slave Trade. The Scottish MP Henry Dundas proposed an amendment which inserted the word "gradually" in the motion. So the House of Commons pledged to "gradually abolish" the British Slave Trade.

"How Sir! Is this enormous evil ever to be eradicated, if every nation waits till the agreement of all the world shall have been obtained? There is no nation in Europe that has, on the one hand, plunged so deeply into this guilt as Great Britain, or that is so likely, on the other, to be looked up to as an example."
William Pitt, Prime Minister, 1792

In 1806 Wilberforce called upon his brother-in-law and fellow abolitionist James Stephen to help him with the legal arguments for drafting a bill. Stephen had spent much of his youth in Aberdeenshire with his Scottish born parents and grandparents; he had attended Aberdeen University and was greatly influenced by his Scottish lecturer James Beattie, the evangelical academic and opponent of the trade and slavery. As a lawyer associated with Parliament he had been posted to St Kitts in the Caribbean in an official post. He was horrified by the treatment of the enslaved and described a slave trial as violating 'every principle' of law.

On his return he wrote abolitionist pamphlets. It was his careful legal drafting and the closing of potential loopholes in the legislation that went to Parliament that helped to make the 1807 Bill a success when it was finally passed in Parliament in February 1807.

Credit: Image of the sale of estates, pictures and slaves in the Rotunda, New Orleans, from *A Tribute for the Negro*, by William Armistead. A copy of the book is held by Glasgow City Libraries.

International Turning
Opinion (1807 – 1838)

For the enslaved the period of 1807 to 1834 was one of the most difficult. It had been believed by many campaigners that an end to the trade would mean that the existing enslaved would be treated better as there was no longer an endless supply of new Africans being brought in.

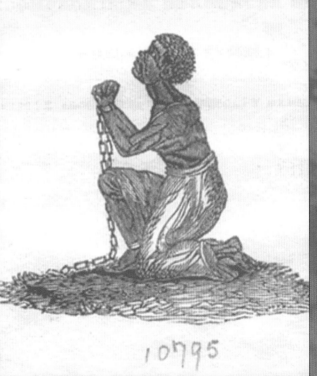

Credit: Title page of the Wrongs of Africa, by Miss MB Tuckey. This is a book of anti-slavery poems published in Glasgow in 1838 (Glasgow City Libraries).

Chapter 7: Turning International Opinion (1807 – 1838)

The Royal Navy and Policing Abolition

The 1807 Abolition Act made the slave trade illegal for British ships and subjects. However it did not outlaw slavery itself. The Royal Navy was given the task of patrolling the coast of West Africa. This 'West Africa Squadron' was based at Sierra Leone. It stopped British ships to see if they carried enslaved Africans. If caught, ships could be confiscated and their masters fined.

The Africans were returned to Africa and released, usually in Sierra Leone, not necessarily their place of birth. The decision by Britain to end its involvement in the slave trade did not mean it ended completely. Other countries continued slaving and Britain attempted to stop this trade by policing the seas, applying military and diplomatic pressure and by giving bribes.

For Africans the end of the slave trade in the British Empire did not mean the end of trade with Europeans. Just as before the trade in humans had started, goods suitable for the European market were produced, in particular palm oil. There were a number of valuable trading goods with West Africans such as spices, woods and woven clothes. Palm oil was the most profitable and could be used in consumer goods such as soaps and as a lubricant in machinery during the Industrial Revolution.

Slavery Continues But Unrest Spreads

For the enslaved the period of 1807 to 1834 was one of the most difficult. It had been believed by many campaigners that an end to the trade would mean that the existing enslaved would be treated better as there was no longer an endless supply of new Africans being brought in. However, that was not the reality; instead, harsher restrictions than ever were introduced to ensure that slave numbers did not fall. The opportunities to buy freedom became non-existent and the female slaves were subject to yet more sexual demands from the plantation owners with the intent of breeding new slaves.

As a result more rebellions and uprisings took place amongst the slaves. The Christianisation of the enslaved that had occurred towards the end of the 18th century meant that they demanded to be treated equally with other Christians. Furthermore, many of those missionaries who had converted the enslaved had also taught them to read and write, thus they were able to read about the campaigns that were happening back in Britain. This encouraged the enslaved to mount their own resistance.

The organised Jamaican uprising of December 1831 led by Samuel Sharpe, an informally educated and highly religious enslaved man, was a severe blow to the authorities and the pro-slavery lobby. Sharpe organised a passive strike that turned violent and the island militia was mobilized. 500 of the enslaved were killed either during the reprisals or afterwards as a result of trial. Samuel Sharpe was hanged in May 1832 for leading the strike. The uprising resulted in two Parliamentary inquiries and helped bring forward the end of slavery.

After 1807 many of those who had campaigned for the end to the trade, such as Zachary Macauley, turned their attention and their initiative to ending slavery completely in the British Empire. Many more organisations were set up. The petition campaign started again, with Scotland alone sending nearly 1,000 petitions to Parliament in the early 1830s.

However, key to achieving their aims was the Parliamentary Reform Act 1832, which meant that different people were now elected to Parliament and the franchise itself was extended to include some of the middle classes who had long campaigned against the trade and slavery. The Anti-Slavery campaign culminated in 1834 with the abolition of slavery throughout the British Empire. Initially a system of 'apprenticeship' that continued to restrict personal freedom was introduced. Complete freedom for all enslaved peoples was finally granted in 1838. The enslaved people were free, but no consideration was given to compensating them for the years that they had been denied their freedom.

On the other hand, to achieve abolition, preferential British sugar tariffs were introduced to allow plantation owners to survive into the 1840s. £20 million was also paid in compensation to slave plantation owners in the West Indies – over 40% of the national budget, the equivalent of $2.2 billion today (around £1.12 billion).

(Adam Hochschild, *Bury the Chains: The British Struggle to Abolish Slavery* (London, 2005), 347)

Credit: Chasing a Slaving Dhow near Zanzibar, 1876-77 (w/c on paper) by Ross-Lewin, Rev. Robert (fl.1877) © Private Collection / © Michael Graham-Stewart / The Bridgeman Art Library Nationality / copyright status: English / out of copyright

The Legacy:

Scotland, Britain and the Caribbean

When addressing the history of slavery, and discussing the horrors that occurred, it is often mentioned that 'not all plantation owners were cruel' and that some 'treated their slaves fairly'.

View of tobacco ships at Port Glasgow, on the west coast of Scotland, in the mid-1760s. Tobacco was unloaded here and taken to the Broomielaw, the main harbour of Glasgow at that time, by small vessels (Glasgow City Libraries).

Chapter 8: The Legacy: Scotland, Britain and the Caribbean

The legacy of the slave trade is still very much in evidence today, in the people that live in our communities, in the attitudes we have to human rights and political campaigning, in the names we have given to our streets and our buildings, and even in the documents held in our local archives. In our homes we listen to African Caribbean inspired music, we eat foods from around the world and we have mixed lineages all around us. Descendants of formerly enslaved people have Scottish surnames or ancestry.

The legacy of England's and Scotland's participation in the slave trade on the Caribbean and the Americas is equally visible there, in the street names, the dominance of the English language and the family names of those who still live there. In Virginia there is the community of Scotland in Surry county. Whilst in the Caribbean there are Scottish surnames as well a Scottish Branch of the Masons in McGregor Square, Kingston.

The journey from the slave trade to the bicentenary of its abolition was not easy. Some of the ideas embraced during that period such as racism, prejudice, stereotypes and denial of truths have remained within our societies. Nevertheless, by using the 2007 bicentenary of the abolition of the slave trade as an opportunity to be better informed, we can acknowledge and accept our shared histories.

When addressing the history of slavery and discussing the horrors that occurred it is often mentioned that 'not all plantation owners were cruel' and that some 'treated their slaves fairly'. This might well be the case, but it does not change the key fact that it was deemed acceptable for one group of people to own another group and deny that group its freedom. The 2007 bicentenary is an opportunity to continue the work started by Macauley, Wilberforce and others and end slavery in the modern world, whilst remembering the past.

Bibliography and Sources

Olaudah Equiano, *The Interesting Narrative and Other Writings* (London, 2003)

Madge Dresser, *Slavery Obscured: The Social History of Slavery in an English Provincial Port* (London, 2001)

Richard Hart, Blacks in *Bondage: Slaves who Abolished Slavery* (Jamaica, 1980)

Richard Hart, *Slaves who abolished slavery, vol. 2 Blacks in Rebellion* (Jamaica, 1985)

Adam Hochschild, *Bury the Chains: The British Struggle to Abolish Slavery* (London, 2005)

Alan L. Karras, *Sojourners in the Sun: Scottish Migrants in Jamaica and the Chesapeake, 1740-1800* (Ithaca and London: Cornell University Press, 1992)

Edward Long, *The History of Jamaica, or General Survey of the Ancient and Modern State of that Island* (London: T. Lowndes, 1774), 3 vols; vol. 2

P.J. Marshall, ed, *The Oxford History of the British Empire, vol. 2 The Eighteenth Century* (Oxford, 1998)

'The sharer of my joys and sorrows': Alison Blyth Missionary labours and the female perspectives on slavery in the mid-nineteenth century Caribbean. (Paper presented at the 'Empires of Religion' Conference, University College, Dublin, June 2006, by Dr John McAleer)

Kenneth Morgan, *Slavery, Atlantic Trade and the British Economy, 1660–1800* (Cambridge, 2000)

J.R. Oldfield, *Popular Politics and British Anti-Slavery: The mobilisation of Public Opinion against the slave trade, 1787-1807* (Manchester, 1995)

Mary Prince, *The History of Mary Prince* (London, 2000)

David Richardson, *The British Empire and the Atlantic Slave Trade, 1660-1807* in *The Oxford History of the British Empire, vol. 2 The Eighteenth Century,* edited by P.J. Marshall (Oxford, 1998)

Mimi Sheller, *Consuming the Caribbean: From Arawaks to Zombies* (London, 2003)

Hugh Thomas, *The Slave Trade: The History of the Atlantic Slave Trade, 1440-1870* (London, 1997)

James Walvin, *Questioning Slavery* (London, 1996)

Websites:

www.portcities.org.uk

www.understandingslavery.com

www.nationalarchives.gov.uk

www.nas.gov.uk

www.bbc.co.uk/london/features/abolition

Websites with further information on the slave trade and its commemoration:

www.infoscotland.com/noplace/slavetrade

www.ltscotland.org.uk/abolition

www.direct.gov.uk/slavery

www.communities.gov.uk

www.culture.gov.uk/about_us/culture/abolition_of_slavetrade_bicentenary

www.understandingslavery.com